Project Polar Bear

Jennifer Nault

Weigl Publishers Inc.

Editor
Diana Marshall

Design and Layout
Warren Clark
Bryan Pezzi

Copy Editor
Heather Kissock

Photo Researcher
Tina Schwartzenberger

Published by Weigl Publishers Inc.
123 South Broad Street, Box 227
Mankato, MN 56002   USA
Web site: www.weigl.com

Library of Congress Cataloging-in-Publication Data

Nault, Jennifer.
 Project polar bearnew / Jennifer Nault.
   p. cm. -- (Zoo life)
Summary: Showcases the development and growth of a baby polar bear at a zoo, discussing the zookeeper's role in its life and the natural habitat, foods, and life cycle of the animal.
 ISBN 1-59036-014-1 (lib. bdg. : alk. paper)
 1. Polar bear--Infancy--Juvenile literature. 2. Zoo animals--Utah--Salt Lake City--Juvenile literature. [1. Polar bear. 2. Bears. 3. Animals--Infancy. 4. Zoo animals.] I. Title. II. Zoo babies (Mankato, Minn.)
 QL737.C27 N38 2002
 599.786'139--dc21

                    2002006394

           Printed in the United States of America
           1 2 3 4 5 6 7 8 9 0   06 05 04 03 02

Photograph Credits
Every reasonable effort has been made to trace ownership and to obtain permission to reprint copyright material. The publishers would be pleased to have any errors or omissions brought to their attention so that they may be corrected in subsequent printings.

Cover: baby polar bear (John Warden/MaXx Images); **Corel Corporation:** pages 11 right, 16, 17 middle, 18, 21, 22 bottom, 23; **Bryan Pezzi:** page 7 left; **John Warden/MaXx Images:** pages 13, 17 left; **Jameson Weston/Utah's Hogle Zoo:** title page, pages 3, 4, 5 left, 5 right, 6, 7 right, 8, 9, 10, 11 left, 12, 14, 15, 17 far left, 17 right, 17 far right, 20, 22 top; **Anna Zuckerman-Vdovenko/ MaXx Images:** page 19.

Contents

A Baby is Born

It was a night in mid-December when something wonderful happened at Utah's Hogle Zoo. Soft cries came from the polar bear **enclosure** as a mother polar bear gave birth. No one witnessed the birth because it happened in the middle of the night.

Zoo Issues

Should newborn baby animals be put on public display?

At birth, the polar bear cub weighed slightly more than 1 pound.

The next morning, **zookeepers** visited the polar bear enclosure. They saw a baby polar bear cuddled up against her mother. The little cub's eyes were closed. With help from her mother, the newborn climbed onto her mother's chest to **nurse**. The cub had pink skin under her thin, white fur. She could not walk, but she could crawl. During her first checkup, the cub was **vaccinated** and weighed.

The mother polar bear and her cub were kept in a quiet enclosure. Zookeepers wanted to keep the cub away from public view until she was old enough to swim and move around without difficulty.

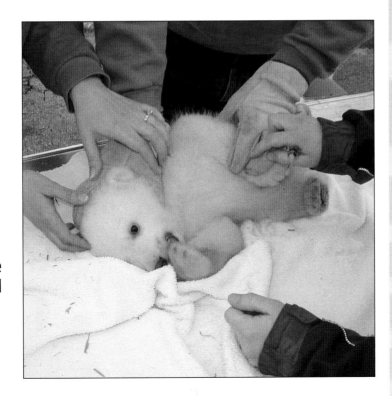

■ In February, the polar bear cub had her first checkup. At 2 months, she weighed more than 12 pounds.

Meet the Baby

The zoo decided to hold a contest to name the baby polar bear. Animal lovers across North America came up with more than 2,500 different names for the cub. The name Anana was finally chosen. *Anana* means "beautiful" in the **Inuit** language.

Zoo Issues

Should baby zoo animals share enclosures with their mother? Why?

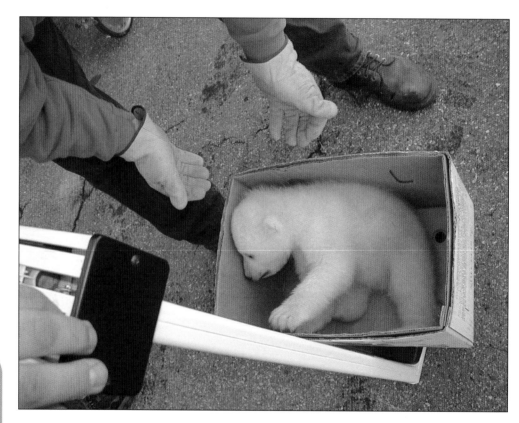

During her first few months, Anana looked like a live teddy bear. She could fit inside a small cardboard box.

- The polar bear's natural **habitat** is in the Arctic. This area is known for its cold temperatures and snow. It includes northern parts of Russia, northern Norway, Greenland, northern Canada, and northern Alaska.

- At 3 months old, polar bear cubs weigh from 22 to 26 pounds. By 6 months, male cubs weigh about 90 pounds, and female cubs weigh about 80 pounds.

- Polar bear cubs learn to walk at about 8 weeks of age.

Although Anana is very curious, she never strays too far from her mother. To stay safe, she is guided by her mother's sounds.

During her first month, Anana's eyes opened to the world. At 2 months of age, Anana's white, fuzzy fur became thicker. She learned to walk. Her **canine teeth** also began to grow.

Anana's mother stayed close to her newborn cub. By 2 months of age, the cub began to explore her enclosure. At 3 months, Anana showed interest in the large pool. Her mother encouraged her to swim by pushing her into the water and showing her how to move.

Swimming for Seals

Polar bear cubs learn many life skills while they are growing up. In the wild, mother polar bears teach their cubs what to eat, how to hunt seals, and how to stay safe on the ice. Since Anana was born in the zoo, she did not need to learn to hunt. Instead, she learned similar skills by catching balls and playing with logs. She also learned to swim. At first, Anana avoided the water. Before long, much of her day was spent splashing in the pool.

Whenever Anana is in the water, her mother is always nearby to make sure the cub is safe.

Zoo Issues

Why is it important for zoo food to be similar to animals' food in the wild?

BRAIN BOOSTERS

- The polar bears at Utah's Hogle Zoo are fed by the zookeepers. The basic polar bear diet consists of frozen fish and a special polar bear mixture, which is similar to dog food.

- Sometimes, the polar bears are given fish and fruit that have been frozen inside blocks of ice. This helps keep the polar bears active.

- When a mother polar bear hunts **prey** in the wild, her cubs stay near the den until she returns. If her cubs become noisy, the mother may swipe at them with her paw. This teaches the cubs to be silent. They watch her so they can learn to hunt.

- In the wild, polar bear cubs stay with their mother until they are about 2 years old. Often, they hunt with a brother or sister until they are ready to travel alone in their **territory**.

Zookeepers bring food to the polar bears once a day. From this routine, Anana learned a skill that polar bears in the wild do not. She learned to move out of the way before zookeepers enter her enclosure. When zookeepers bring her daily food, Anana knows to move into the holding area. This allows them to safely enter the enclosure to distribute the food and clean Anana's home.

During mealtimes, Anana is protective of her food. She will not even share with her mother.

Meet the Parents

Anana's mother is named Chinook. Her father is called Andy. They are both captive bred, which means that they have never lived in the wild. Chinook was born at Memphis Zoo in 1977. She was transferred to Utah's Hogle Zoo in 1997. Andy was born at Buffalo Zoo in 1989. He was moved to Utah's Hogle Zoo to mate with Chinook as part of the zoo's **breeding program**.

Zoo Issues

Should breeding in zoos be controlled and monitored?

Since polar bear cubs nurse until they are 2 years old, young Anana and Chinook must live in the same enclosure.

Anana has four **siblings** and five half-siblings living in other zoos. Anana's siblings live all around the world, from New York to Japan. The youngest siblings, twin brothers named Alcor and Mizar, were born in 1998.

Like polar bear parents in the wild, Anana's parents did not stay together to raise her. Instead, they spent just a few days together during mating. Anana's father did not help raise the cub.

■ Although polar bears spend most of their lives alone, mothers and their cubs form close family units.

- Male polar bears fight for females during the mating season, which lasts from April to May.

- Female polar bears are ready to mate at about 4 years old.

- In the Arctic, a pregnant polar bear builds a birthing den to keep her cubs safe from the cold. She digs the den out of a hard-packed snowdrift. Inside, the den is very warm. In winter, the temperature inside the den may be 40 degrees warmer than the air outside.

Chinook Warms Up to Andy

Zookeepers slowly introduced Andy and Chinook. At first, the two polar bears sniffed each other through a small opening between their separate enclosures. The polar bears liked each other.

The two polar bears shared an enclosure until Chinook was ready to give birth. Then, she was moved to a birthing den. It was similar to the one she would have made for herself in the wild. Male polar bears pose a threat to cubs. So, Chinook and Andy were kept apart after Anana's birth.

When Chinook and Anana are in the public area of the polar bear enclosure, Andy is kept in his private enclosure.

Zoo Issues

Think of some reasons why zoo animals may need to be separated.

BRAIN BOOSTERS

- The American Zoo and Aquarium Association (AZA) keeps records of zoo animals. These records show how many animals live at each zoo. The AZA monitors polar bear breeding. It makes sure that the number of polar bears born in captivity does not become too large to manage.

- Adult male polar bears may fight polar bear cubs. They are so **territorial** that they may even kill their own cubs.

- Cubs watch, follow, and imitate their mother until they are ready to live on their own.

Polar bears have different personalities. Since Anana was raised apart from her siblings, she likes to get her own way. Anana has even been **aggressive** with her mother. Anana is more vocal than the other polar bears at Utah's Hogle Zoo. She makes many sounds to communicate with her mother and her zookeepers.

The Zoo Crew

Zookeepers feed and care for the polar bears daily. Zookeepers also educate the public about polar bears and related **conservation** issues.

The polar bear enclosure at Utah's Hogle Zoo has a waterfall and a pool for swimming. These features copy the polar bear's natural habitat. Zookeepers know that the right features and foods help keep Anana and Chinook healthy and happy. During winter, the enclosure becomes very cold and snowy. The temperature is often similar to the polar bears' natural habitat.

Zookeepers clean the polar bears' home every day. They also help design, build, and repair the enclosure.

Zoo **veterinarians** use their polar bear knowledge to keep Anana healthy. They vaccinate her against diseases, prescribe medicines, and treat wounds. They can also set broken bones and perform surgery if necessary.

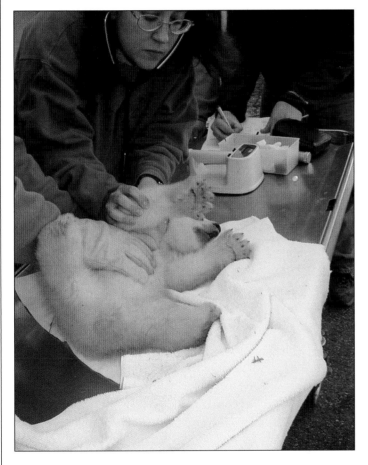

■ Regular checkups monitor the cub's growth. The checkups help keep Anana strong and healthy.

HOW CAN I BECOME A ZOOKEEPER?

While a zookeeper's education may vary, a college degree is often required. Degrees in zoology or biology are preferred. Sometimes, animal care experience can be as desirable as a degree. Volunteering at a zoo or a veterinary clinic is a great way to gain animal experience.

ZOO RULES

People do not realize that they have an effect on the animals living in a zoo. The polar bears at Utah's Hogle Zoo watch visitors and respond to different scents and sounds. The polar bears pay special attention to their zookeepers, since their arrival often means food. Zoos have rules that help keep animals and visitors safe and healthy.

Utah's Hogle Zoo's Rules:
1. Always stay with the group.
2. Do not climb on or over the fences.
3. Do not feed the animals.
4. Do not harass the animals.
5. Help keep the zoo clean.

Animal Gear

Polar bears have features that set them apart from other bears and help them survive in the cold. From thick, heavy fur to long, strong bodies, polar bears are designed for Arctic winters.

Zoo Issues

Why should zoo enclosures be similar to an animal's natural habitat?

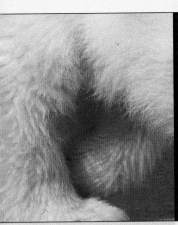  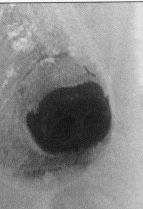 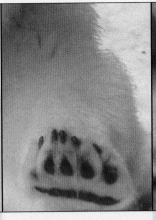 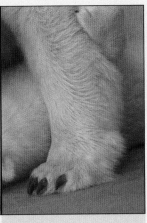

Fur
Polar bears have two layers of fur. Their outercoat is made of long, coarse hair. Their undercoat is denser. It keeps polar bears warm in very cold temperatures. It may look white, but polar bear fur is colorless. This helps the fur heat up in the light of the sun.

Teeth
Polar bears have longer, sharper teeth than other bears. Polar bears are carnivores. This means they only eat meat. Their long canine teeth allow polar bears to tear off thick chunks of seal meat and **blubber**.

Nose
Polar bears have a very keen sense of smell. The polar bear's nose helps track down mates. It also finds seals' breathing holes. Polar bears can smell seals up to 40 miles away.

Paws
Polar bears have large paws. They measure about 12 inches across. Their paws stop polar bears from sinking into the snow. The hair between their toes and the rough, black pads on the bottom of their paws help polar bears walk on slippery ice.

Claws
Polar bears have five sharp, curved claws on each paw. Each claw is about 2 to 3 inches long. Their claws help polar bears catch and kill their prey. The claws also help polar bears walk on slippery ice.

In the Wild

In their cold Arctic habitat, polar bears do not have many neighbors. Few animals can live in such cold climates. Polar bears spend most of their lives roaming the sea ice. On the ice, polar bears hunt for ringed seals, which are their favorite food. Much of their time is spent hunting and catching seals.

■ The polar bear's scientific name, *Ursus maritimus*, means "sea bear" in the Latin language.

Seals live in the cold Arctic waters. When the water freezes, seals make breathing holes in the ice. This allows them to come up for air. Above the ice, polar bears use their keen sense of smell to find the holes. When seals come up for air, polar bears pull them out of the water and eat them.

Male polar bears spend most of their lives alone. Females spend most of their lives raising their young. Sometimes, polar bears will form groups called sloths during summer.

■ Younger polar bears are more likely to form a sloth than older polar bears.

Room to Roam

Polar bears use more territory than any other land animal. In zoos, polar bears do not have as much space as they do in the wild. Today, zoos all over the United States, including Utah's Hogle Zoo, are working to improve polar bear enclosures. One of the zoo's first projects will be to add more water features to the polar bear enclosure.

Zoo Issues

How can zoos help wild animal populations?

Utah's Hogle Zoo plans to give its polar bears more room. It also wants to offer more play activities and areas away from public view.

BRAIN BOOSTERS

- In 1973, five nations came together to protect polar bears from **over-hunting**. Denmark, Norway, Russia, the United States, and Canada drew up the International Agreement on the Conservation of Polar Bears.

- Zoos often take in young polar bears that have been **orphaned** in the wild. In a zoo, orphaned polar bears receive proper care and a safe place to live.

- In the wild, polar bears can live 15 to 18 years. In zoos, polar bears can reach 30 years of age.

- Egyptian King Ptolemy II owned the first captive polar bear. He kept the polar bear in his private zoo in Alexandria, around 265 BC.

Wild polar bear populations have been threatened by over-hunting. Since the 1970s, efforts have been made to limit the hunting of polar bears. As a result, the number of polar bears living in the Arctic has grown. Today, the wild population is stable.

Polar bears are also threatened by **global warming**. The Arctic climate is warmer than it once was. This means that less ice covers the sea. Polar bears hunt for seals, their main source of food, from the sea ice. When the ice melts, it is harder for polar bears to catch seals.

Today, there are between 22,000 and 27,000 polar bears in the wild.

Polar Bear Issues

Benefits of Zoo Life

- No danger from over-hunting, competition, or habitat loss
- Regular food, play time, and medical care
- The public is educated about polar bears
- Is easier to research polar bears in zoos
- Breeding programs maintain a stable zoo population
- Can live a longer life

Benefits of Life in the Wild

- More natural space in which to hunt and live
- Maintain diverse polar bear populations
- Daily mental and physical challenges, such as hunting
- Part of the natural web of life consisting of plants, predators, and prey
- Live complex life
- Maintain independence

Folk Tale

The Polar Bear Son

An Inuit legend tells the story of the meeting between a lonely woman and a polar bear. One day, a woman finds a polar bear that has lost its mother. She takes it home and raises it. Soon, her neighbors discover the polar bear. They are afraid of the polar bear and decide to kill it. When the woman finds out, she helps the polar bear escape. To thank the woman for her kind actions and respect for animal life, the polar bear takes care of her for many years.

Source: Dabcovich, Lydia. *The Polar Bear Son: An Inuit Tale*.
New York: Clarion Books, 1997.

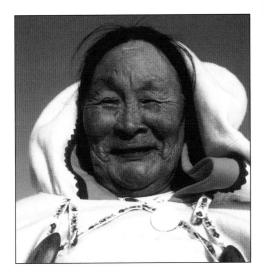

More Information

The Internet can lead you to some exciting information on polar bears. Try searching on your own, or visit the following Web sites:

American Zoo and Aquarium Association (AZA)
www.aza.org

North American Bear Center www.bear.org

The International Association for Bear Research and Management (IBA) www.bearbiology.com

Utah's Hogle Zoo www.hoglezoo.org

CONSERVATION GROUPS

There are many organizations involved in polar bear research and conservation. You can get information on polar bears by writing to the following addresses:

INTERNATIONAL
World Wildlife Fund
International
Avenue du Mont-Blanc
CH-1196, Gland
Switzerland

UNITED STATES
Great Bear Foundation
P.O. Box 9383
Missoula, Montana
59807

Words to Know

aggressive: forceful and protective
blubber: layer of fat below the skin
breeding program: producing babies by mating selected animals
canine teeth: four long, pointed teeth, toward the front of the mouth
conservation: the care and monitoring of animals and animal populations for their continued existence
dens: shelters of wild animals
enclosure: closed-in area that is designed to copy an animal's home in the wild

global warming: an increase in world temperature that leads to climate change
habitat: place in the wild where an animal naturally lives
home ranges: areas where an animal normally lives and travels
Inuit: Native-American group that lives in the Arctic
nurse: drink a mother's milk
orphaned: left without a mother
over-hunting: hunting an animal population to the point where its numbers become greatly reduced

prey: animals that are hunted and killed for food
siblings: brothers or sisters
territorial: fighting to protect and defend one's territory
territory: area that an animal will defend as its own
vaccinated: given medicines to prevent diseases
veterinarians: animal doctors
zookeepers: people at a zoo who feed and take care of the animals

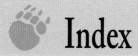

Index